The Smart & Easy Guide to Small Business Plans: How to Write a Successful Small Business Plan for Your Startup Company

Richard Norris

Legal Stuff

Copyright Information

Copyright © 2013 Checkmate Marketing Group LLC. All rights reserved worldwide.

No part of this publication may be replicated, redistributed, or given away in any form without the prior written consent of the publisher.

Checkmate Marketing Group LLC

Earnings Disclaimer

EVERY EFFORT HAS BEEN MADE TO ACCURATELY REPRESENT THIS PRODUCT AND IT'S POTENTIAL. IN TERMS OF EARNINGS, THERE IS NO GUARANTEE THAT YOU WILL EARN ANY MONEY USING THE TECHNIQUES AND IDEAS IN THIS MATERIAL. INFORMATION PRESENTED ON THIS BOOK IS NOT TO BE INTERPRETED AS A PROMISE OR GUARANTEE OF EARNINGS. EARNING POTENTIAL IS ENTIRELY DEPENDENT ON THE PERSON USING OUR PRODUCT, IDEAS AND TECHNIQUES.

ANY CLAIMS MADE OF ACTUAL EARNINGS OR EXAMPLES OF ACTUAL RESULTS CAN BE VERIFIED UPON REQUEST. YOUR LEVEL OF SUCCESS IN ATTAINING THE RESULTS CLAIMED IN OUR MATERIALS DEPENDS ON THE TIME YOU DEVOTE TO THE PROGRAM, IDEAS AND TECHNIQUES MENTIONED, YOUR FINANCES, KNOWLEDGE AND VARIOUS SKILLS. SINCE THESE FACTORS DIFFER ACCORDING TO INDIVIDUALS, WE CANNOT GUARANTEE YOUR SUCCESS OR INCOME LEVEL.

ANY AND ALL FORWARD LOOKING STATEMENTS HERE OR ON ANY OF OUR SALES MATERIAL ARE INTENDED TO EXPRESS OUR OPINION OF EARNINGS POTENTIAL. MANY FACTORS WILL BE IMPORTANT IN DETERMINING YOUR ACTUAL RESULTS AND NO GUARANTEES ARE MADE THAT YOU WILL ACHIEVE RESULTS SIMILAR TO OURS OR ANYONE ELSES. NO GUARANTEES ARE MADE THAT YOU WILL ACHIEVE ANY RESULTS FROM OUR IDEAS AND TECHNIQUES IN OUR MATERIAL.

Limitation of Liability

THE MATERIALS IN THIS BOOK ARE PROVIDED "AS IS" WITHOUT ANY EXPRESS OR IMPLIED WARRANTY OF ANY KIND INCLUDING WARRANTIES OF MERCHANTABILITY, NONINFRINGEMENT OF INTELLECTUAL PROPERTY, OR FITNESS FOR ANY PARTICULAR PURPOSE. IN NO EVENT SHALL OR ITS AGENTS OR OFFICERS BE LIABLE FOR ANY DAMAGES WHATSOEVER (INCLUDING, WITHOUT LIMITATION, DAMAGES FOR LOSS OF PROFITS, BUSINESS INTERRUPTION, LOSS OF INFORMATION, INJURY OR DEATH) ARISING OUT OF THE USE OF OR INABILITY TO USE THE MATERIALS, EVEN IF HAS BEEN ADVISED OF THE POSSIBILITY OF SUCH LOSS OR DAMAGES.

Table of Contents

The Way to Write a Business Plan 6
Giving the Proper Name to Your Business 9
Tax Deductions for the People Who Own Their Own Business 12
Increasing Business Capital by Convertible Debt 15
Start-Up Financing and Government Programs............................. 18
Eight Inexpensive Ideas on How to Start Your Business............ 21
Eight Methods to Grow Your Business 24
Eight Methods for Raising Funds for a New Start-Up 28
Alternative Ideas for Raising Funds for a New Start-Up 32
Five Aspects to Consider Before Going for Business Capital 35
Why Create a Business Plan? 38
The Information to Add to the Front Cover of the Business Plan
 41
Great Tips on Formulating Business Projections......................... 44
The Most Important Aspects to Incorporate in a Business Plan
 47
Why Include a Competitor Analysis in Your Business Plan? 50
Ongoing Work: Why It Is Important to Update the Business Plan
 53
Sample Business Plan Outline 56
We Want Your Feedback on This Book! 58

The Way to Write a Business Plan

When writing a business plan, one of the most important things to think about is the plan's financial statement. Some other significant aspects involve the mission statement of the company, the name, market analysis, plan of the organization, goals of the company, and the evaluation of the competition.

In the majority of cases, the business plan ends with the financial section. This is the section which tells people about the marketability of your idea and how willing investors will be to invest in your company. There are several elements included in the financial statements. The most important sections include the income statement, balance sheet and a cash flow projection. Besides these elements, you should also include a short analysis of the financial statements.

There are two categories of expenses that you will have to include in the financial statements. These two categories are the operating expenses and the start-up expenses. The start-up expenses include licensing, business registration and permit fees. You also have the possibility to include the rent and inventory deposits along with the rental or purchase of operating equipment.

A business' operational costs include the salaries and benefits of the employees, mortgage or rent, expenses with raw materials, utility payments, maintenance, and office supplies. These costs depend on the specific aspects of your company. In the majority of cases these expenses are projected over a period of 3-5 years.

Another aspect that the business plan has to cover is a description of the industry that your business will operate in and its position within that industry. In this section you will have to include estimated sales over the past couple of years and the size of the industry.

Some other aspects that you will have to cover include the economic and national trends that influence the industry and its general outlook. This means that you have to determine the chances of succeeding in the industry and the impact your company will have on the industry.

In the next section you should offer demographic information on the prospective clients of the business. You will have to address their sex, age, lifestyle, education, income level. You may also add additional information such as the motives of the customers, their occupation and the way they spend their free time.

It may also be interesting to address the kinds of equipment that the customers use which are related to the products that you sell. As an example, if you are selling memory cards for cameras, you should know the number of people who buy products of this kind. You can find out this information by surveying people or by analyzing statistical data.

When you do research regarding your prospective clients, you will get some proof of the earning potential of your own company. This will be an important piece of information when you will start looking for financing for the business. In the same time this document will ensure you and the investors that there will be a return on the investments made. If you do other research or analysis, you should include it as well in your business plan.

An evaluation of the possible competition is the key to having a successful business plan. This way you will be able to pass by the marketing barriers and in a short while be able to start your business. It is important to include in the business plan the ways that you are planning on promote your products. In this part of the business plan you should focus on the way your products or services benefit the customers. If you have several services or products, you should give details of all of them.

Another section of the business plan could involve the management and operation goals. You should also give details of the organizational structure of the company. In this section you will address some of the legal aspects of the business and you should also mention the physical location of the company. Include all details that you think are important for convincing investors that you have a workable plan.

If you think that you can't provide all this information or that you can't present the information in a convincing manner, you might want to use the services of professionals. You could hire a consultant or work with a non-profit organization. Fellow associates might also help you if contacted.

Giving the Proper Name to Your Business

It is more than challenging to find the perfect name for your business. This is a name that people should remember and that is suggestive for your activity area, regardless of whether or not you have a logo.

There are several aspects to consider when choosing the name. Firstly, the name that you choose must be memorable and it should be easily spelled. It is difficult for people to look up a name in a directory if they don't know how to spell it. They may get to pages that they aren't interested in if you don't choose a name that can be easily found.

It's not enough for the name to be memorable and easy to spell; it is best if it has a visual quality too. For instance, if you have a restaurant called "Sandwich Queen," when people see it they will instantly think about a woman dressed in an elegant gown, holding a sandwich in her hands. (If there is a restaurant with this name, it is a mere coincidence and it is not related to this article.)

It is of upmost importance for the name to have a positive connotation. This may be quite difficult, because many of the words have both positive and negative connotations. However, there are some words, such as "queen" that have a positive meaning, because people usually think about the status a queen has and her beauty.

It is good for the name of the business to be short and relevant for the products that you are marketing. However, sometimes it is difficult to find a name that is both short and suggestive. In case you would like a simple name, you could use your first name, like "Julie's Soups." This way the customers will imagine a real person selling soup. Another idea is to name the business "Julie's Homemade Soups" making the customers think that the soups are fresh and hot. Generally speaking, the names that are more than three words long are too long for people to remember.

In case you would like to give people more information than the information given by the name, you could do so in the advertisement campaigns. In other cases, you should stick to the 2-3 words of the business' name. Besides this, it is important for the name to have a meaning even without a logo so when people hear about the business they will be able to visualize the meaning of the name.

Although, as it has been mentioned before, the name should have a meaning on its own, it is a good idea to add a logo as well. The logo is a piece of art that symbolizes the core purpose of the business. This can be placed above, below, or alongside the business name. Make sure that the name and the logo come with colors that look good together.

The name should be everything that has been mentioned before, but it also has to be original. If you use your first name, it is possible that someone else used the same name too. This means that your name won't be truly original. If you find an alternative way to send the same message, you will get more points when it comes to originality.

In case you find it difficult to find a name that fulfills all the requirements mentioned until this moment, you should consult a professional. A good idea to find a name for your business is to do some research about the existing names that people know about. If you observe the names of well-known fast foods, hotels, or grocery stores, you will surely see a pattern.

When people feel like they need some help regarding their business decisions, they seek professional help. Even the most experienced businessmen and businesswomen need some help from time to time. Finding the most suitable name is the most important aspect of starting your business.

Tax Deductions for the People Who Own Their Own Business

If you already have a business, you may know that the costs of owning a business are quite high these days. For sure you know from the start-up you have to watch every penny spent because you don't have any certainty yet. Probably you also know about the taxes that you, as a business owner, will have to pay.

The good news is that there are some methods to decrease the taxes. Usually these costs are returned to you in the form of tax deductions. New start-ups can take advantage of these deductions.

The most common deductions include transportation expenses and operating expenses. The operating expenses involve the costs of maintenance, mortgage, rent, labor, phone bills, internet services and others. The transportation expenses include the travel miles and the costs of repairing a vehicle.

The provisions of deductions in case of home businesses and small businesses vary according to your location. For example, in many states the number of miles is multiplied by a certain amount of money per mile to determine the gas mileage of vehicles. Another option is to deduct the repair expenses. However, in the majority of states business owners can deduct only one of the two.

Some other expenses that business owners have to pay include hotel charges, client's lunches, speaking room rentals, and seminar fees. If you fly by plane or rent a car you can deduct these expenses as well. It is a good idea to talk to your tax advisor to find out about other expenses you can deduct from your taxes.

We can say that if a service or product that you buy helps the expansion and operation of the company, it is considered tax deductible. This is meant to be an incentive for business owners to spend money in order to make their business grow.

If you trust your business, the money spent on operating expenses will return to you. You shouldn't consider the tax deductions as a means to an end. However, the majority of the business owners take advantage of them to make sure they will be able to make a profit next year.

There are some people who abuse these tax deductions to gain more income. As an example, some business owners buy luxury cars for their "business" that they deduct from their taxes but that are rarely used for the business. In other cases people buy more supplies for their "business" which are later used in their personal life.

For instance, it is misuse of office supplies if you buy paper for the business but end up using the paper for writing letters to your family and friends who don't have internet access. Another example is deducting luxury vacations as business trips.

The rules of tax deductions vary according to your location and they can also change from one year to the other. If you are an honest business owner, you can use the tax deductions to decrease your expenses, which is important during the first few years.

In case you aren't certain whether a tax deduction is legitimate or not, you should talk to a tax advisor. Also make sure to read the instructions you were given when you received the tax forms.

Another tax deduction is getting the business involved in charity. Usually this is a legitimate deduction. If you take part in fundraising activities, the business will be rewarded with tax deduction. Again, in case this isn't clear to you, you should talk to a professional.

Increasing Business Capital by Convertible Debt

There are two main ways of raising capital for a business: debt capital and equity capital. Debt capital means that the money is borrowed and the business engages itself to pay it back. In this case there is an interest rate that is to be returned in a given period of time.

Equity capital is provided by the share owners to maintain the functioning of the business and it doesn't have to be refunded. It is possible to turn the debt capital into equity capital.

Mutual stock is the easiest equity capital to get. There are numerous identifying components accepted by mutual stock:

• There is no possibility to change the mutual stock into another kind of protection;

• They can be given by one individual only in one ballot;

• The incentives have no boundaries unless these are announced by the managers;

• In case of a settlement, the stock holders can decide on how to disperse the assets.

There can be two kinds of mutual stocks. This is what you have to look for when searching for capital. One of them is the Class "A" mutual stock. This is something like the preferred stock but there are no exceptional rights.

The other kind of stock is the junior stock. This is seldom used by businesses, but it is faster and more inexpensive.

The decision of the kind of capital you will get is an important one and you also have to decide on how to organize the funding when it comes to stakes. It is also important to get a company consultant to advise you when you start a capital-gaining operation.

The GT Business Plans helped business owners come up with over 200 business plans. These business owners raised a total of over $750 million in funds, they released many new kinds of merchandise and they created new competition. GT Business accepts venture capital firms, corporations, angel investors, and also entrepreneurs.

The venture capital firms are concerned by the various components that lead bankers to their decisions when giving money to a business owner. Although the financial institutions are facing hard times, they already have their standards of proceeding. While the financial institutions are creditors, the venture firms become the owners of a business.

These firms buy the stocks of the business thus immobilizing their own funds. This is why it is important for them to analyze the services and products of the business. They usually work with businesses that offer a fast return and that have high earnings. The venture capitalists are more interested in the characteristics of a product than the financial institutions.

It is difficult for venture capitalists to assess the productivity of a new start-up. This is why they need insurance as to the proposition size, rating and necessities operations, and the period of time for which the business has been around, to decrease the chances of a loss.

Almost all the investment involvement of these firms is confined by the plans that the business owners offer them. They usually prefer those businesses that have a high growth potential and that can introduce new merchandise to the market.

The venture capitalists are looking for a big and fast profit instead of having smaller incomes over a longer period of time. They examine the information provided for at least a period of five years. This is because there are a lot of start-ups that are looking for funding. Venture capitalists are professional people who know all about business and they can find problems even if you think your business plan is perfect.

Start-Up Financing and Government Programs

A lot of people are dreaming about having their own business, not having a boss and having financial freedom. Nonetheless, this can't be achieved without financing. People can apply for loans or look for financial backers. If they aren't successful with this, they can apply for a credit card. There is another route as well: government funds.

The U.S. government is the only one offering loans and grants to new start-ups, especially in the case of small businesses. There are a lot of available funds if you know where to look. The government does this in order to strengthen the economy and to offer social benefits.

In many states there are development agencies and local governments that are willing to finance new businesses. Normally the funds can be used for financing any kind of business. The plans are easily approved. All it takes is for you to be an American citizen of at least 18 years of age. There is no need for credit checks, security deposits or collateral. Things couldn't be easier.

One way to find out whether you can apply for such grants is to visit grants.gov. This website has been used by thousands of business owners looking for funding for their business. On the website you will find thousands of grants from 26 agencies. You will certainly find someone willing to offer you a grant.

Another place you can look for financing is the Small Business Administration. This agency specializes in small businesses and they can help you find a government agency with suitable financing criteria. Although this agency doesn't offer loans, they can point you in the right direction.

The Small Business Investment Company can also help you find grants. Although you may have never heard of it, it might be the agency you have been looking for. It is the result of a partnership between investors and the U.S. government. Although it is privately owned, it has strong connections with the government and it can help people find capital through government loans and grants.

Believe it or not, this is the service that Apple Computer, America Online, Federal Express, Callaway Golf, Outback Staples, Gymboree, and Sports Authority all used to finance their start-ups. We can say that these are some of the most successful companies of the moment. This shows you that government funds may turn out to be invaluable for your business.

Another advantage of using the Small Business Investment Company is that every dollar will be matched by the Small Business Administration, which will help you even more. There are a lot of specialized grants offered depending on various factors.

When looking for government loans and grants, this might be the best place to start. Minority-owned businesses can also help you raise funds. The National Association of Investment Companies can turn out to be a great help. This association deals with minority owned companies.

Military veterans have additional funding options. In this case you could get in touch with the Small Business Self-Employment Service. This belongs to the Small Business Development Center and the President's Committee on Employment of People with Disabilities. Both are willing to offer grants to disabled veterans.

As you can see, it doesn't matter whether you are an average person, a member of a minority, or a disabled veteran – the government has resources to help you. Obtaining such funds may be easier than getting a traditional loan. You shouldn't waste any more time because there are billions of dollars waiting to be claimed to help you own the business of your dreams! You just have to find the right funding.

Eight Inexpensive Ideas on How to Start Your Business

The truth is that it's not easy to start your business when you're on a tight budget. If you are serious about your plans, there are some inexpensive ways to get things started. Here is a list of eight ideas on how to set up your business.

1. Have a home office. This is one of the best ways to start an inexpensive business. A lot of people started with home offices and some of these businesses have become large corporations over the years. This way you won't have to pay a rental fee.

2. Get an online store. An online store is a lot less expensive than a traditional store. Another advantage is that you can increase the customer base without having to think about additional space. The customers have no problems with paying for shipping if the prices are low enough and so you could have customers from all over the world. You will be able to offer a wider product selection if you don't need a store and use only storage space.

3. Advertise online. If you have little money, internet advertising is just perfect for you. There are a lot of inexpensive ways for you to reach people. As an example, you can get the word out by pay-per-click ads, which cost as much as you are willing to pay. The good news is that you can determine your budget with these ads. You can also buy website traffic that costs as little as a few dollars per month.

4. Make connections on the internet. There is also the possibility to interact with prospective clients on forums, blogs and other discussion boards. This way people will get to know you and your business. You can also reach people online through SEO (or search engine optimization). This means adding articles to your website that contain keywords that people usually use to search on search engines.

There is also the option of expanding the income potential by choosing keywords to use in articles that don't really have any market competition. This way you can make sure that it is your site that will pop up first on the search engine pages.

5. Make use of the local community. In order to get the word out, you should interact with people from your community. You can meet new people at social gatherings, outdoor parks, churches, or at work. If the business isn't in conflict with your community, you could always mention it in a casual conversation.

6. Get the word out. You could print out some fliers and distribute them to businesses and homes. This is a fast and cheap way to let people know about your business. If you have satisfied customers, they will tell other people about your services. People will always tell other people and at a point there will be no need to spend any more money on internet or paper advertising. Word of mouth is the cheapest way to advertise a business.

7. Give people promotional items. You could have some magnets, notepads, coupons, erasers, or buttons with the name and logo of your business and you should give these to people. This kind of advertising is less expensive than television, billboard or radio advertising.

8. Buy used or wholesale items. In order to save some money, you should think about buying wholesale items. Another option is to buy used products. Also think about the fact that you can save some money if you buy large quantities of given products. This is useful when you need office supplies or business furniture.

These are only some example of starting a business with a tight budget. It is important to be as thrifty as you can without affecting the quality of products or services sold.

Eight Methods to Grow Your Business

If you are reading this article, it means you want to make the most of your business. Here are eight ways that will help you make the business bigger than you ever expected.

1. Let people know about the business. Your business cannot grow if people don't know about it. Business owners who are on a tight budget might want to consider business cards and flyers. In some cases business owners can participate in social activities to make themselves more visible. Some other forms of inexpensive advertisement include magnetic signs, buttons, T-shirts, leader boards and so on.

Another thing you should think about is creating a customer base by phone calls and communicating with prospective clients. These will talk to other people about your business and thus the news will travel by word of mouth.

If you have a larger business, you will need large-scale advertising. A lot of companies use the radio, billboard signs, television and newspapers to make themselves more visible to the people who might be interested in their services.

Internet advertising is suitable for both big and small businesses. It is a good idea for businesses to set up a website where they can advertise themselves and take orders from their clients. The internet could do wonders for your business.

2. Be cautious. In order to have a successful business, you will have to use many different tools. Nonetheless, you should make sure that you don't go overboard. As an example, if you have an income of $1,000 at the moment it would be foolish to rent an office for $900 a month. If this is something you need, you would be better off buying a building or applying for a loan.

Although you might think that you don't have the resources for these, the payments could turn out to be a lot lower than you expected. As a rule of thumb, once the business starts bringing you income, you should save about a third of it because later you might need the money. Naturally, you will have to spend money to set up the business, but you shouldn't waste it.

3. Make wise decisions regarding the business tools. In many cases you can see advertisements of products and tools that people claim you can't succeed without. This usually isn't the case. Before you make a purchase, you have to think about how you can use the given tool. Since there are a lot of tools that you need, you should make sure to avoid the ones that you don't.

4. Ask for professional advice and help. If you aren't sure about what to do in a given situation, you should ask for professional help. You ought to be looking for the help of people who have been operating a business like yours with success. These people have real experience and they already know the mistakes that you can make. If you listen to their advice you will be able to avoid the pitfalls of leading a company.

5. Delegate the chores. If you would like to succeed with what you started, you should hire someone to do the "dirty" work. As an example, you may hire an accountant to deal with the financial aspects, a mechanic to perform maintenance for the equipment, or find a cleaning service. You should focus on the things that you are good at. Naturally you will have to pay the people who are working for you and you have to make sure that this is a good investment for the business.

6. Get some loans and grants. There are a lot of ways for you to finance the business if you don't have the funds yourself. You could be thinking about corporate loans, small business loans, and government grants, among others. This is especially important in the case of new start-ups. No matter what you would like to do, you can be sure that there is a way.

7. Be open towards your customers. The key to having a successful business is to maintain good relationships with customers. The requests of customers have to be fulfilled as soon as possible and you have to be able to offer the services you promised. If you happen to make a mistake you have to make sure that you do it right. Don't forget that the "customer is always right."

It is just natural that after a while the business won't be able to keep up with all the customers' requests. This is the moment when the business needs a service representative. This person needs to know as much as possible about the products or services. Besides this person you might also need customer service staff, who will look after the business. This way the customers will know that they will get in touch with someone who knows the business.

8. The relationship between price and quality. It is not imperative to sell the products or services at the lowest price on the market. Nonetheless, it is important for the price and value of the product to be comparable. If the quality you offer is high enough, the customers will come back, even if the price is slightly higher than average. Of course they will also come back if they don't have to pay a very high price for the products or services that they get.

These are pieces of advice that you can use regardless of whether you would like to open a new unit or you would like to have more customers. However, they don't take the place of receiving help from a professional consultant. If you need help, all you have to do is search for a consultant in your area online.

Eight Methods for Raising Funds for a New Start-Up

You will need a lot of energy for your new start-up. You might be surprised about the amount of work you will have to do in a relatively short period of time. Computer consultants, since they are only concerned with the technical aspects of the start-up, tend to focus only on the technical parts of the business. The best thing you could do is to assess your abilities and accept the help of people who have corresponding abilities.

When starting a new business you have to think about the 90/10 principle. This means that you have to focus 90% of your resources on merchandising and the remaining 10% on technical issues. There are four activities that should take up 90% of your time:

• Research;

• Propagation of principles;

• Taking trips for sales;

• Making propositions.

The main goal of yours is supposed to be gaining eminent customers. In the remaining time you will have to address management issues, face establishment obligations and not forget about communicating with the people around you and doing research. As the new business gets on the right track, all these things will require less and less of your time. At this point you should focus on getting customers.

All you have to know about a new business start-up

As it has been mentioned before, you will have to remember the 90/10 principle at the starting point of your business. About 90% of your time should be sacrificed for business growth and commercialization and the rest of your time should be taken up by technical acquisitions.

If there are no customers for you to demonstrate your technical skills to, there is no point in wasting time with this aspect. This is why you have to remember that the most important aspect of a business is its customers.

A lot of people already saw that this aspect is entirely true. It doesn't really matter what you wish to do but rather what activities will bring you income. You will find the saying "cash flow is master" more than true in the case of your business.

There are a lot of things happening when a business is started and all this could become overwhelming for the owner. There are product promoting points that you have to go to, taking part in the governing body, supervising the production, hiring new people, monitoring the employees, marketing, and most importantly, assessing the success of the marketing campaigns.

It is interesting to know that there are a lot of business owners who have absolutely no idea about where their money is coming from and where it is going. While at the beginning this doesn't seem to be a big problem, later you will see that it will become difficult to keep track of everything. Here are eight tips to secure the ways to gather money:

• People invest money in tasks and products and not your company. This is why you will have to remind them that there is a charge for the given product or service.

- Bad cash fluctuation isn't always visible. For this reason you have to make sure that you keep track of everything that enters and leaves the business. If you have a long-term project that you need to get a loan for, you should make sure that you add to the price the cost of the loan as well (which is also known as the interest).

- If you buy raw materials which you need to pay for in 30 days, make sure that the customers pay even before you have to make the payment because this way there will be no need for bringing in external funds (like a loan).

- In order to be able to make estimations of future cash flow, you have to make sure that you have constant production and that you won't have to recall any of the products. In some cases the customers may say that they need more time to pay you. In this case you have to require the payment in a firm but polite way.

- If you have cash flow problems, you could get a line of credit at a financial institution that you are working with. This way you can reduce the costs of capital. In case you have any overnights in your cash flow, this can be covered by the credit line. However, this is only a short-term solution. You have to remember that there are interests you will have to pay and you shouldn't use a credit line unless it is unavoidable.

- Factoring is another possibility for you to get some money now. This means selling your accounts and cashing in sooner. Again, there are charges for factoring which can vary from one company to the other.

- It is important to make sure that if you get some help, the results will offset the investment that you make.

- Although these measures for getting cash may seem appealing to you, you should make sure that you get only the services that you really need so that you won't have unnecessary expenses.

It is of the upmost importance to take cash flow seriously because it can improve the company or ruin it. If you are planning on making any changes, you should write them down and start calculating. In case you make a mistake you will certainly learn from it, but it is best to avoid making mistakes. Cash flow is one of the best tools you can use.

Now you know why the cash flow is so important. Sometimes keeping everything in mind might turn out to be complicated. You may want to talk to a professional about this aspect and do some research on how you could optimize your expenses.

Alternative Ideas for Raising Funds for a New Start-Up

It is difficult to start a new business on a low budget. If you don't have perfect credit, things could become even more difficult. However, there are some creative ways for you to increase your funds. All business owners ought to know that there are a lot of non-profit organizations that offer to provide funds for different kinds of start-ups.

In order to start and run a business you will need business capital, which means money and resources. You will use some of this money to buy manufacturing equipment, merchandise stock, office supplies, and to pay employee salaries. There could be some unplanned expenses as well, such as property insurance.

It is possible that you don't qualify for a business loan and in this case you will have to find other methods to finance your business. Some of the possibilities that you have include government loans and grants. Maybe you won't have to pay back a part of these. However, these work something like the bank loans, so there will be a waiting period.

Naturally, you will also have to come up with a business plan. As you may have thought, the grants or loans with no interest are usually given by nonprofit organizations so this is something you could think about if you can't get a bank loan.

It doesn't really matter whether you apply for a loan or a grant, either way you will need a business plan. The money could be coming from the U.S. government or the government of your country or from private sources, such as nonprofit business organizations.

According to your locations, you may qualify for loans or grants given to certain categories of business owners. As an example, some national and local government agencies offer grants and loans to people belonging to minority ethnic groups like women or African American people. In other cases, grants are given to the business owners in economically challenged neighborhoods.

In case you are interested in grants and loans of this kind you should use the internet to search for them and you will certainly find a few that you qualify for. Books can also give you some good ideas and you can find them for relatively small fees.

Business owners may not know about all the possibilities that they have regarding loans and grants. If this is your case you might be interested in the services of a grant counselor. Usually you will have to pay a fee to this professional and he or she will lead you through all the steps of finding the suitable grant for you. Also, they can grant you access to a database containing grants and zero interest loans.

If you apply for a grant or for a zero interest loan, besides the business plan you will also have to submit a grant proposal. These proposals can be easily written with the help of specialty books or the Internet. Naturally you can also hire someone to write it for you. Everything depends on the purpose of the grant which is the same as the purpose of your business.

The type of organization you are dealing with determines the process of applying and receiving the grant or loan. At the same time, the funds available also vary from one year to the other. Although it takes quite some time and energy to find suitable grants and loans, you can be sure that it will all be worth it.

In case you would like to know how to create a business plan, it might be a good idea for you to approach a nonprofit organization that offers funds. There are also a lot of websites that offer sample plans and advice in this matter. In the majority of the cases it is important to include in the business plan the projected incomes and losses over a five-year period.

If you have expansion plans or plans for hiring employees, you should include them in your business plan. Besides these, you will also have to mention business needs, like office furniture.

The business owners who have good plans will be able to apply for funds to meet the financial needs of the business. Although it might take some time to find the right funding, you will be glad you invested so much time in it.

Five Aspects to Consider Before Going for Business Capital

It is difficult to start a new business. There are a lot of things to take into consideration. The first thing you will need is a well-considered business plan. If you have this plan you will be able to increase your chances of finding the other elements that you need to kick-start your business. The next thing you must have is capital. So how should you get started and how to find investors/lenders? Here are five aspects that investors/lenders take into consideration before they invest in or lend to a new business.

The first thing they consider is the exit strategy. Although this is something you never thought about, this is the first aspect they think about. Most probably you didn't think about this until now, but it is important for investors to know the long-term direction of the business.

Usually the investors would like to gain ten times the amount they invested in five years. One of the most common exit strategies is acquisition. This means that at a point in the future a bigger company buys your business. As an example, Google bought Web 2.0. Some other possibilities include liquidating or going public. Don't forget that it is hard data that persuades investors and this is why you should do some research.

Some other aspects that researchers will be looking at are the entry barriers. This means the ways to prevent other people from entering the market and stealing your ideas. Did you ever think about this possibility? Are you prepared for such situations?

Examples of entry barriers involve legislations, patents, and the uniqueness of a product. If there are strong barriers, it will be more difficult for competitors to enter the market with a replacement of the product that you are selling and thus you will be able to have a greater market share of the market you are operating in. This will bring greater profits and your business will seem more appealing to possible investors.

While you should do everything you can to keep competitors away from your business, you should be able to point out to the investors some similar services or products. This is important because the investors should know how well such products do on the market. As a result they will have more confidence in your business. Although being different gives you an edge, the investors will want to see some proof that your idea will actually work.

Investors, especially venture capitalists will want to know whether you have funds for starting the business. This is a form of protection for you especially if you are working with venture capitalists to make sure they won't own the majority of your company in the end. Having some revenue will keep the company in your hands. Naturally the investors are most interested in how much money you need and what you need it for.

In order to answer all their questions, you will have to do a lot of research. For you to know the amount you need, you will have to research everything that you have to buy to know the prices. You will have to take into consideration even the smallest items. If you are accurate, you can save a lot of trouble for all parties involved. This way you will know what you will spend the money on. Investors and lenders are looking for well-thought-out plans. When approaching a lender you should have a complete financial plan. Don't forget to add the operating expenses, marketing expenses and legal fees to the list.

Now that you know all about the aspects to consider before approaching a lender, you can expect to have some success. It is good to know that it will cost you a lot of research and hard work, but you can be sure it will be worth it. You have to have a thorough business plan that follows the mentioned guidelines and you will have the necessary funds faster than you would have thought.

Why Create a Business Plan?

It is a well-known fact that it is impossible to predict the success of a business. However, if you can come up with a good plan, you will be prepared for the ups and downs of your business.

Business plans are needed regardless of whether you have a partnership or a sole ownership. If you have a good plan, you will be able to communicate with others who would like to know more about your business. Don't forget that the business plan is also a tool that can convince the investors and lenders that you have a workable plan.

Preparing a business plan can protect you from investing in a business that won't bring profits; it is meant to analyze your idea. In order to create a proper business plan you will have to do a lot of research.

The kinds of research you will have to do vary according to the stages of planning. You will have to look at the annual reports of the companies that offer similar products and services, use test markets, and conduct surveys.

Another advantage of writing a business plan is that you will have to think about the costs related to running a business. This way you will find out whether or not you will be able to raise funds for starting the business and whether or not you will be able to maintain your activity in the long run. If you find out that you don't have enough capital to run the business, you will know that you have to raise more capital to keep the business running.

Another aspect that you have to consider regarding the business plan is that you will have to come up with the goals and the purpose of the business. Besides these, you must decide the kind of company that you want to have. For example, you might want to start marketing a new bicycle brand or open a new pet store chain. Keep in mind that if you have a business plan, you will have higher chances of succeeding.

In case you have to write a business plan for a company that exists with the purpose of expanding the business, you can also include graphs, charts and tables with the business data. Also, think about statistics that you could include like the revenue you earned during the first year or for a long period of time, if that company has been around that long. It is also important to give information regarding profits and losses and the increase of revenue from one year to the other.

There are some other benefits as well that you might be interested in. If your goal is to attract investors, they might be interested in the products and services you offer. Presenting a good plan will increase your chances of attracting investors and they will be more likely to agree to finance your activities.

In order to gather information you could buy some books, visit agencies, or visit some websites that offer sample business plans. In some cases you can find templates for free and you can save them on your computer to personalize and edit.

The length of a business plan depends on the kind of business we are referring to and the amount of details that you would like to give the investors or lenders to help them better understand your business. Usually there is an introductory part first that includes the name or names of the owners and basic information about the business. Then you should add the mission statement. After this include the financial results of the business for the previous year (except in the event that you have a new business).

In case you are preparing a business plan for a new business, you might want to include financial data from another company if you have access to such information. You should be looking for evidence that will show that you have a workable and marketable idea. If you can't find information on the financial data of a company with similar products or services, you should include information from a test market.

Once you manage to show that there is a potential for earning a profit, you should include projections of earnings and loss. This is the perfect place to tell a little something about the goals of the business. There is no exact order that you should follow with your business plan, but the experts prefer this format.

There are market research experts and consultants who you could hire to help you come up with a business plan that will be appealing to investors. There is also some software that is meant to create business plans. It doesn't matter whether you would like to expand the company or just make more money each month; it is a must for you to come up with a business plan.

The Information to Add to the Front Cover of the Business Plan

Professionals say that you should write the first page of the business plan last. This is because it should contain a summary of the business plan that you came up with.

It is important for the front cover to include the name of the (future) company and its location. It is also a good idea to add the contact information of the company executives. Then you should have a couple of sentences about the different aspects of the business.

Other aspects that the front cover should include, besides the ones already mentioned, are the mission statement and the names of the members of the management. Since this is a summary of the plan you wrote, you should wrap up the plans to determine the customer base, competition analysis, marketing ideas, financial plans, and operational expenses.

It is important to keep everything short on the front cover – which shouldn't be longer than two pages. You can use a bullet list format, paragraph format, or outline format. The format you choose depends on the target audience.

If you are only handling an internal plan, you can go for a less formal format, such as using paragraphs. However, if you would like to show the business plan to investors and lenders, you should make the plans as appealing as possible.

Investors find it important to easily identify and understand the different aspects of the business. Don't forget that the business plan can determine the success or failure of your business. It can also determine the expansion of the business. The more effort you put in creating the business plan, the more pleased the readers will be and they will take you more seriously.

It is vital not to have any spelling errors in the business plan and to avoid grammatical errors. This is especially important in the case of the front cover of the business plan.

Usually the first page is the cover page and the summary of your work is supposed to be on the second page. However, if you are going for a simpler format, you can have the summary on the first page as well. Even though you may be going for a simple design, it is alright to add some colors to the cover page to make it more pleasing to the eye.

Adding a bit of color will make the business plan more attractive. Adding the logo of the business is also a good idea. However, you have to remember that the graphics shouldn't be the center of attention.

It is important to make sure that all the information, data and figures on the cover page are accurate. Also try to be as honest as possible in the statistical summaries that you add to the front page. Naturally you have to focus on honesty and accuracy in the entire document. In case you present false information, you could be penalized and most probably you won't have any chance to receive the funds you need. It is possible that your actions will have other legal consequences as well, and this is something you want to avoid.

If you really want to succeed with your business, you should start writing the business plan as soon as possible. The tips mentioned before will help you create the perfect cover for your plan and the ideas will be as concise and as clear as possible. In case you feel like you need more information on the topic, you should read some specialty articles. The good news is that there are a lot of resources to help you in this matter.

A lot of business owners turn to professionals to help them come up with their business plans. These professionals can help with the calculations too. If you're not good with writing, you can pay someone with good writing skills to write it for you. No matter who creates the business plan, you have to make sure that the cover is perfect.

Great Tips on Formulating Business Projections

Business projections are difficult to formulate without the help of a professional. These professionals can help you with all the aspects of writing a business plan and they have experience with making projections of profits, losses and costs of a business.

If you are planning on starting a new business, the specialists will be able to tell how much each aspect will cost you. The expenses that you will have to take into consideration include marketing, research, operation and production. Other costs to be thinking about involve shipping, utilities, communication and transportation. It is a good idea to take into consideration the mortgage or rent of a property too, along with the company benefits and salaries of the employees.

In case you have never done anything of the sort before, you might want to ask the help of a professional to make the projections for you. Usually the professionals say that business owners shouldn't invest more money in a business than they are willing to lose. Besides this they will also be able to tell you how to promote the business to avoid failure of the business.

In order to come up with projections, you will have to calculate the amount that you can produce and the price at which you would like to sell your products. Then multiply the price by the amount sold in a year. This is one way to make profit projection. Naturally you can't know precisely how much you will sell, but this is something an expert can help you with.

One way to gather information is to conduct a survey involving potential customers. If you involve the potential customers in the process you will have a more accurate idea on how much you can sell. Naturally not even the surveys are 100% accurate but they are used by a lot of successful companies and so you can use them as well.

Another option to project profits is by analyzing the statistics of other companies who handle products and services just like yours. You can use this idea in the case of products and services marketed with success by other companies. The downside of entering a market with a lot of competitors is that your product will need an added bonus compared to the other products on the market. Normally the markets that come with a lot of competitors also have high demands, so the companies find it easy to succeed.

As an example, you might know that fast food chains are always popular, no matter how many of them you can find in a given area. This is because people need variety in their nutrition and they don't want to eat at the same place over and over again. This is why restaurants don't mind being near each other, because they know they will still have traffic. Another good example is janitorial services. No matter how many companies are competing against each other, there will always be a need for cleaning crews.

If you talk to such companies you will find that the janitorial companies don't want to accept small jobs that require only 1-2 hours of work. If you start a business of this kind, you can be sure that you will be able to make enough money to live happily ever after. However, you will require several clients that need your services on a daily basis. Freelance writing is something like this as well. Writers can always find a job because the demand for their services is very high.

Another idea to consider regarding making projections is to think about the revenues and costs of the previous year. In order to calculate the profit that you had, you have to sum up all the income you had and all the expenses you incurred. Once you do this, you will have an idea about how much money you can make in the following year.

The more people know about the business, the money you will be able to make, so you should prepare to make more money in the second year than in the first one. This happens because the customers you had in the first year were pleased with your services.

In order to determine income and expense projections, you might need the help of professionals. If you search the internet, you will surely find someone to help you.

The Most Important Aspects to Incorporate in a Business Plan

Even the most successful businesses are based on a well-researched plan. A good business plan gives answers to all the questions any investors or lenders could have about your business. Here is a list of the possible questions and the answers you could give to them.

Why did you start the business? This is something you have to be certain about or you will find it difficult to get the funds that you need. The clearer the purpose of the business is, the higher your chances are of receiving the funding. I your business plan is written in a clear manner, it will be easier for the investors and lenders to understand the main purpose of the company.

Besides this, the future employees should also know why they will work for you. Common purposes of the company include helping retailers and customers to complete their tasks or to diminish their workload.

Another answer is to educate children or to enhance the creativity of adults in a given community. No matter what purpose your company has, it has to be stated clearly so that everyone can understand it.

What kind of service or product will you sell? In this section you should describe every detail of the product or service you offer. You have to mention the function of the service or product. In case you have several products and services you will sell, you will have to write about each of them.

Is there a market for the business and what is the target group? It doesn't matter whether you wish to enter an existing market or you would like to create a new market; it is a must for you to have some market research. This way you can be sure that there are people who are willing to buy your products or services.

It is a good idea to clearly indicate the target market that will be available to buy your products. There are several ways to find out about this information. Usually people start by analyzing annual reports of companies operating on the same market and by conducting surveys.

How do you want to go through with your plan? This is an important question to ask yourself because you can be sure that other people will ask you as well. It doesn't matter how many different products you have, the question is how you will go on marketing them.

How much does it cost to run the business? In order to answer this question you have to calculate all the production and operation costs along with the marketing and creative costs of the business. You will have to spend money on factory equipment, desks, office phones, buildings and property. Naturally you will have to pay communication bills and utilities. It will also cost money to find out the potential of the business and let's not forget about marketing costs either.

What kind of equipment and materials will you need? In order to run the business you will need equipment that will produce the products or services and supplies. You have to make a detailed list of all the things you will need to offer high-quality products or services.

What goals does your business have? To succeed with your company you have to be clear on what goals the business has. As it has been mentioned before, it is imperative to include projections in your business plan and think about a time period of 3-5 years. Besides this it is also a good idea to include communication and management goals to improve the products and services. The more goals the company has, the more success it will have.

You can talk to a professional to help you come up with a business plan or you can read articles that will help you in this matter. Sometimes the business plan also includes other aspects, like the charts with last years' earnings, especially if the company is in an expansion phase. The more information you have about the growth potential of the business, the more likely you are to find funding for it.

Why Include a Competitor Analysis in Your Business Plan?

Although it may seem overwhelming to analyze the competition, you can be sure that it is worth it. Finding out information about the competitors can turn out to be invaluable information for your business.

First of all, you will have to find out who the competitors are, including the direct and indirect competitors. There are different ways to do so, both online and by looking around in your area. Nonetheless, the best thing you could do is to pay a visit to your competitors. During this visit you should gather as many details as you possibly can. You should know a little something about their prices, services, their target customers and anything else that could help you.

Another thing you could try is to talk to customers to find out what they think about your competitors. You may also pose as a customer of the competition and buy a product or service from them to find out exactly what you are competing with. This way you will get a better sense of the business and you will see how the competition treats their customers.

Once you are done with all this, you just have to analyze all the data that you have gathered. This will help you find the weak spots of the competition and also their strengths. At the same time you will find the areas that you cannot compete with. As a result you will see how you could improve the performance of your company and what areas you have to work on to eliminate its weaknesses.

In order to be sure that you can use the strengths, you have to set realistic goals which are cost-effective and that meet or fulfill a need of your company.

Some business owners may ask how the competitor analysis helps their business. Such an analysis will help ensure you are a step ahead of the competition. It will help you avoid mistakes that other business owners make such as wasting money and time with marketing that doesn't bring results, targeting the wrong customers, offering products that don't meet given needs, or applying incorrect prices.

It is important to conduct a competitor analysis at the start-up or whenever the business changes. If you have a new business, you should take advantage of everything that a competitor analysis can offer. Since there are so many competitors these days, analyzing them has become a necessity. Another reason to perform the analysis is that all companies are getting more creative and they are all using the latest technology; it is a must to know what others are up to.

There are a lot of reasons for you to o an analysis of the competition. For example, an analysis of this kind can assure you that you are always one step ahead, making changes even before the market changes. This can really make your business boom. Another reason is to be able to predict the changes that the competition might undergo. This way your business will be able to meet the needs of the customers before any other company.

Naturally one of the main advantages of the analysis is that you can use it for learning. There are a lot of aspects you will learn about with the help of a comprehensive and complete analysis of the competition. As an example, you can find information about the past successes and failures of your competitors. By knowing about these, you can also find out why they happened to make sure that you won't make the same mistakes as your competitors.

An analysis of this kind will enable you to learn about products and technologies that are essential to the industry. Maybe one of the competitors uses something that helps them very much. If you didn't have the analysis you couldn't have known about it and you would have been at a great disadvantage.

There are many other reasons for you to conduct an analysis. For instance, you could make good mergers and acquisitions in the future. All in all we can say that a good analysis can ensure your success on the market.

Ongoing Work: Why It Is Important to Update the Business Plan

It is good to have a business plan when you start the business, but you also have to remember that the market is dynamic. Once the market changes, you have to make sure to update the business plan to ensure that things will run smoothly. If you gain knowledge in the field or information about new technologies, it can greatly influence your business plan if the changes affect the results of the business.

The areas that you have to consider are varied and so it is not enough to only consider the beginning of the business. You also have to consider the current status of the business plan. There are several points of view to consider, such as the administrator's point, institution description, commercial criticism, management and establishment, sales and merchandising management, financial petitions, commodity or assistance lines, and also funding. These are the main points, but there can be others as well based on the market that you are operating in.

One of the most important things to update is the mission statement, which you can find in the administrator's point. This can change as the business grows. This is the statement that says what the business is all about and what its commitments are. Changing the mission statement as the business grows will show the customers that you have an ongoing work and the business makes adjustments to serve their needs. If you have happy customers, you will make more money.

Don't forget that the plans of the company are based on possible future events. There is no way to predict these events precisely and so you should update these plans to make sure that the projections are close to reality. If you have an old business plan it could cause you to fail because it isn't in line with reality. By updating the business plan you can see whether you reached your goals or not.

Even if the business plan seems to be working for the moment, most probably it won't reach its full potential. Usually people don't update the business plans because they are comfortable this way. However, this might become a problem. It is possible that you will be able to keep some customers, but you won't be able to acquire new ones and thus the business cannot grow. By updating the business plan you can help the business evolve.

Another good thing about updating the business plan is that you can see the big picture more clearly. This plan is an important business tool to gain an overview of the company. If you focus on the day-to-day problems you may not see the big picture. If you do see the company as a whole you can make adjustments to improve its results.

If you change the company globally you will save time by not having to change one department at a time. If you update the business plan you will be able to see the warning signs of business and financial risks.

In case you are behind in the sales of the first half of the year, if you update the business plan you will be able to anticipate the losses even before they occur and you can make adjustments. The same thing is true in the case of business risks.

Another thing that an updated business plan can help with is the employees. If your plans are updated you will be able to give information to the employees about the direction of the company. This way they will see that their actions affect the entire company and they might become more productive. While updating a plan is a lot of work, you can be sure that the results will be worth all your trouble.

Sample Business Plan Outline

Following this paragraph you will find a sample business plan outline. This is a general outline you can use as a template for your own business plan. As you put it all together, be sure to modify to suit the needs of your particular business. Some sections may not apply and you may have to add other sections or subsections to fit everything in. Always remember that this is YOUR business. Everything needs to be built around your vision. That being said, this outline is a very good place to start and will give you a solid framework to guide you.

1.0 Executive Summary
1.1 Mission and Vision
1.2 Financial Objectives
1.3 Start-Up Summary

2.0 Products and Services

3.0 Market Analysis Summary

4.0 Branding and Marketing
4.1 Competitive Comparison
4.2 Competitive Advantages
4.3 Marketing Campaign
4.4 Exit Strategy

5.0 Management Team
5.1 Personnel Summary and Forecast

6.0 Financial Summary
6.1 Start-Up Funding
6.2 Revenue Forecast
6.3 Break-Even Analysis

6.4 Projected Profit and Loss
6.5 Projected Cash Flow
6.6 Projected Balance Sheet
6.7 Financial Assumptions

Appendix: Year One Financials

We Want Your Feedback on This Book!

Our main purpose is to make sure that our readers get value from the books we publish and that they have a good experience with all of our products. We are always working to improve our books and other products with every revision and update.

Every piece of feedback makes a difference in this process. And we would appreciate yours as well - whether it is good or bad.

Please take one minute to let us know what you thought by following this link:

http://checkmatemg.com/feedbacksmallbizplans/

www.ingramcontent.com/pod-product-compliance
Lightning Source LLC
Chambersburg PA
CBHW071817170526
45167CB00003B/1337